Sheila-Na-Gig Editions

Cover art: Julia WD Harrison
Author photo: John McHone

ISBN: 978-1-962405-80-5

Sheila-Na-Gig Editions
Russell, KY
Hayley Mitchell Haugen, Editor
www.sheilanagigblog.com

# Acknowledgments

Many thanks to wonderful editors of the following publications in which these pieces first appeared, often with different titles or in different forms:

*Appalachian Places*: "Ode to the Autumn Daffodil"
*Appalachian Review*: "Autumn on the Tuckasegee River"
*Literary Heist*: "Hunting Season"
*MIDLVLMAG*: "23 North," "Before Recycling the Beer Bottles at Night's End"
*Northern Appalachia Review*: "Easter Sunday"
*North Dakota Quarterly*: "Sky Burial," "The Mighty Ohio"
*Sprout*: "After the Ice Storm"
*Still: The Journal*: "13 Miles South of Louisa, KY," "Forsaken"
*The Whisky Blot*: "Memories of a Cocktail Waitress Circa 2005"
*Women Speak, Vol. 5*: "Tanya Berry called them *the signs of evil*"
*Women Speak Vol. 9*: "Bad Track," "Lullaby in Lane Three"
*Women Speak Vol. 10*: "Power Dynamic, May 2023"

## Special Thanks

This chapbook would not have been possible without the education, support, and encouragement of so many friends, family, and colleagues. First, a huge thanks to my spouse, John McHone, and my son, Judah, for giving me time and space to write and to Hayley Mitchell Haugen for her belief in and support of my work. So much gratitude also goes out to John Hoppenthaler for taking me on as a student over a decade(!) ago and for the many, many lessons he taught me at ECU (including how to use a damn semicolon) and continues to provide. Many thanks to Doug van Gundy and his excellent Makery classes. To my writing group, y'all are the BEST: Karen Kilcup, Ruth Hoberman, Lucy Biederman, Kathy Goodkin, Jennifer Whitaker, and Sara Backer—many of your suggestions are evident in these poems. Thanks so much to Julia WD Harrison for the one-of-a-kind cover art, and to Tonya Holy Elk, doris davenport, Kari Gunter-Seymour, Joseph Bathanti, Carla Locklear, Emily Kader, and René Locklear White for encouraging me to write no matter what and to not shy away from hard truths. To my MA cohort friends, especially Kevin Dublin, Austin Hart, and Amber Carpenter, thanks for reading so many terrible drafts. To Miller, for the late-night poems on Plexiglass and napkins and for always pushing me to chase my dreams. And for my mom, who sat me down at her Brother electric typewriter one summer afternoon and told me to write poems.

For my mother.
I am forever grateful for your poetic genes.

# Contents

## Labor



## Litter

# Labor

# 23 North

Pete Yorn's *musicforthemorningafter*
pours from the cracked
window of my hand-
me-down Buick with its one
working door handle.

Speakers crackle *I, live on*
*a chain* into the 5 AM
blackness of the interstate
& my coffee. Maybe it'll work

& I'll wake up soon. Another day
picking in the aisles. Match
sticker to item, slap it on, toss
it in the cart. Repeat. Clock

out. Take the interstate
an hour back home. Repeat
tomorrow & Wednesday
& the rest of the work

week. Because there's no
rest for the weary & no
jobs in my hometown
paying above minimum
wage & at least I get

weekends off & am done
before dusk, I tell myself,
avoiding the mass exodus
of 5 o'clock traffic flooding

outward from the city
to the hills & hollers
we call home.

## Bad Track

Early mornings, pre-work or pre-church
or pre-Saturday errands, my mother spackled
her face with Cover Girl's Warm Beige, waved
her magic L'Oréal mascara wand in Deepest Brown
across her eyelids & repeated her regular incantation
into our apartment's only bathroom mirror:
*Man, I look like five miles of bad track.*

My dad fixed track for the C&O in the late
'70s & early '80s. He had long dark hair
then, told me how his boss hated hippies,
how it was always ten degrees warmer or colder
next to all that steel depending on the season,
how he witnessed the gray brains of his foreman's son
spackle the cracks in the track when Junior didn't hear
the engine round the bend. Noises echo in those hills, after all.

They call scars from injecting substances into one's veins
track marks, as though it's possible to track someone's history
through the scars they leave behind. Or maybe these small speckles
dotting elbows & the absences between toes are more
akin to tracking an injured animal, following its bloody sprinklings
until you locate the vacant body. My ex used to walk
to the 84 Lumber yard just across the train tracks
from our small apartment to visit his dealer, coming home
with a bun, enough baggies that he'd be able to lay down track
after track in the recording studio & play enough gigs to get more.

A few years back, a Norfolk Southern train fell off the tracks
in East Palestine without a way to trace the impact
of vinyl chloride, butyl acrylate & isobutylene on the fish,
soil, people who called (& still call) that place home. But it wasn't
the track's fault; instead some faulty rotor or axel or computer
should have functioned properly but failed. There is no person
to blame, no one to call & ask if symptoms should be tracked,
if the water is safe to drink, if the garden can be planted this year.

Home is sacred. No one wants their homes
or lives derailed. We don't want folks
tracking in dirt or dirty laundry; we deserve
safe spaces to examine the islands in our riverine veins,
to utter incantations in our bathroom
mirrors, to sing along to Dylan's *Blood on the Tracks* off-key.

# Memories of a Cocktail Waitress Circa 2005

The men hold their sticks,
chalked at the tips, smashing
balls against one another, ordering

Mich Ultras & Budweisers
& my phone number, tipping me
when they remember as they tip

glass bottles to their chapped, thirsty
lips, puckered like the assholes they are
after the sixth beer settles in their guts.

# Before Recycling the Beer Bottles at Night's End

We had to dump them. Drain
the chaw, its slosh & thick drips

slicking the stained
inside of a repurposed plastic
pickle bucket. Sometimes peeled

labels appeared, their silvers
& reds floating among the back-

wash. The once-white bucket
awash in taffy-brown bottom
dregs, bloated foamy cigarette

filters, flecks of leftover tobacco
sprinkling the surface like stars.

## Autumn on the Tuckasegee River

Translucent white wisps
rise from the murky water,
ghosts of speckled trout
lured in by fly fishermen

who rise from the murky water
like ghosts of their younger selves
lured in by fly fishermen
dreaming of futures unseen.

These ghosts of their younger selves
chase the sun like these men chase trout
dreaming of futures unseen
fleeting hopes, catch & release.

They chase the sun like these men chase trout
exuding power that ends in failure
fleeting hopes, catch & release.
They return empty-handed,

exuding power that ends in failure
but maybe that's the point;
they return empty-handed
because the trout don't belong to them

but maybe that's the point
that nothing belongs to us
because the trout don't belong to them.
We are intertwined, not owners;

nothing belongs to us,
not even the ghosts of speckled trout.
We are intertwined, not owners.
We're just translucent white wisps.

## One for the River Rats

*for Blake*

You steer the barges,
one tattooed hand resting

on the paint-chipped, once-white rail,
the other in control of a ship

bringing shipments of goods
back from Cairo, Kentucky

up the Mississippi shipped
from Panama or China or countries

we greedy Americans can't pin-
point on a map. These goods

we are told are for the greater good,
to ease our troubled lives. Meanwhile

you ease out of your driveway
every three weeks, wave

goodbye in the morning
darkness to only your wife

because the kids are still
sleeping & you don't want to wake

them before shipping off
again, so you steer your truck,

one tattooed hand on the coal-black wheel.

# Leg/Ear

When the doe arrives
tethered to beat-up
pick-up bed or rachet-
strapped to roof rack,

because she lacks
a rack, we'd ask
if we should attach
the tag through her

ear's copper softness
or where the thick thigh
muscle hugs her
downy tail. Our buck

knife sliced a slit no
wider than her eyelid,
just enough to slip
the red plastic

strip through, feed
it back into itself,
ouroboros marking

his territory. A glowing
grandpa once told me
I had no choice. She was
his grandson's first, her

ears dangling sinew; *at least,*
he sputtered, *at least that boy*
*didn't waste any meat.*

# Hunting Season

My right hand held
the thin red plastic
lasso, threaded it

through itself, ringing
the taupe bumpy antler
resembling barren tree

branches. Were sycamore
& elm silhouettes the last
beings this buck or button

buck spotted? Their leaf
litter beneath its tawny
head, autumnal pillows

drenched in blood
the color of dried maples?

## After the Ice Storm

Reenter the woods. Scout
out tinder & kindling. You must

toss the sodden timber back,
but be careful: If you peel

back the bark, you might detect
that moisture doesn't always saturate

the core & you might cast out
a scrap worth keeping.

Learn to snap twigs
between knees & crack

larger limbs over your thick
right thigh bone. You must

cull from felled branches.
Green's no good; it needs
aged so it can know its purpose.

## Exercise

It seems trite that I ask
my students to draw their favorite flowers
when the ridgeline behind my acquaintance is turning to ash

& the streets of Gaza are being bombarded,
bodies scattering like sunflower seeds on the wind
that one student drew & we know

that some bodies like some seeds are destroyed where they lie
but at least the flights of seeds serve
to nourish. Yes, it seems blasphemous for these bodies to be

sketching peonies & poppies when the red of poppy
leaves is being shed in Congo's cobalt mines
by bodies younger than my students.

But in this room, we settle in relative safety, channeling
our inner Monets, sketching pistils & stamens
& petals, paying particular attention to their textures.

This exercise might seem meaningless
when the world is burning & men are murdering
women & the tragedies like bodies keep stacking

& stacking to the ceilings
as these attacks on people & land & planet
seem to be unceasing. Yet my hope in having

these students draw flowers
is that when they see beauty & value in the ugliest of places
that they can enact change, spring up

like defiant dandelions insisting on their presence
alongside a trestle's track.

## Caregiving

I threaten my son's love
of videogames if he refuses
yet again to thrice write

his spelling words & answer
the damn question about how many
bananas three generically-named students
would perhaps have if divided

equally, which we know is not how
the world works, but instead we ask
inane questions rather than shatter a child-
hood sense of justice. The pages stare

him down, their high-contrast letters
threaten his intelligence, heighten his anxiety.
My phone vibrates his worksheets, my mother's love,
my father, discharged to hospice,

an abscess in his lung added to the cancer
& emphysema that are not divided equally
between right lung & left but instead

threaten both & the hospital's answer
is oxygen & morphine. Her words, high-
contrast on my phone's glowing screen
heighten my anxiety, threaten to break

my love for my father & mother & son
into uncountable shards of glass that tear
up my eyelids as I no longer care
about the spelling words or the dinner I planned

that will not materialize to be divided
amongst plates unequally. Perhaps
my son will see his stand-in crackers & cheese

as an injustice while I try to formulate
an answer when he asks *Is Pop okay?*

# Reading Robert Hayden While My Father Visits the Oncologist

*No one ever thanked him,* those mornings my father donned
his decades-old tan Carhartt to tap the rusty Jeep's starter
with the wrench he kept on the tattered passenger floor-
board for such a daily occasion, before he drove the hour,
Columbus-bound *in the blueback cold.* Not on Sundays

like Hayden's father, but my father's paychecks
still *drove out the cold,* monthly payments to Columbia Gas
& AEP & the apartment's rental office making sure
*the rooms were warm.* Our home never shared

Hayden's *chronic angers.* My memories of home
were calm because my father's memories of his childhood
were not. He was able to stop such curses
& trauma but is not able to cease these cells

so hellbent on erasing his memories.
This man & his stories have now become my own
stories, a tale of healing *love's austere and lonely offices.*

## The Cost of Grief

*for Peggy Cory, April 8, 1953-October 5, 2025*

\$3690.93 for cremation, online obituary & grave-
side service with internment. \$800 for junk
removal. \$682.40 for five nights in a hotel

at the bereavement rate with a free
breakfast that included locally baked donuts
from the "original" Crispie Creme (yes, with the C).

\$395 to hire Southern Ohio Monument Company
to carve *2025* to the right of your dash & add
*Nothing gold can stay* below it because you loved

Robert Frost & although my sister & I guessed
your favorite poem was "The Road Not Taken,"
we didn't think it fit the epitaph genre.

\$32 in round-trip West Virginia turnpike tolls.
\$99.91 to the locksmith to unlock the back door
to which no one held the key because it always stuck

& you never opened it. \$26.53 for gas on the way up;
\$28.96 on the way back, because Chillicothe, Ohio
to Millers Creek, North Carolina is mostly uphill.

\$152.60 for the two autumnal wreaths I ordered,
grapevine crescent moons feathered with dried lavender
& orange rounds meant to fill this incessant need

to decorate my two front doors, to dig deep for cheer, to feather
my nest because you can no longer feather yours. My first home,
your body. Your last home—my heart.

## Lullaby in Lane Three

The bespectacled cashier scans my organic raspberries,
pork rinds, avocados, ranch dressing. Her gray bob sways
slightly off-tempo "What's Love Got To Do With It,"
settling into the store from ceilinged speakers, reminding

her & many of us that the hits of our day, like us,
are no longer cool or in fashion. Opposed to this
tune, she hums instead of chatting about the incoming
storm. Her melody of mostly minor keys reminds me

of a lullaby my mother's father hummed to his mother-
less children, a slow short strain, swaying in his throat,
a song my mother recalled from his lips, sacred as a hymn
traveling at the speed of sound to my ears, sleepy

with the buzz of summer's cicadas & the floor fan's
steady pulse. Here, in checkout lane three, the beep
of my butter in the sure hand of Deb, her blue
nameplate reads, evokes blood memories bone deep.

## This is Just to Say

*for William Carlos Williams and Craig Santos Perez*

you have eaten
the peaches

that were on

the tree
& which

I was planning
to preserve

I struggle to forgive
you, squirrels,

for your greed &
your hunger.

# Litter

## Forsaken

We save them—Pack 'n Play, fancy
hiking carrier with removable sunbrella,
GroVia cloth diaper covers
patterned with leaves & clouds. But

now that closet space is needed for grief.

Once our bodies achieve greatness,
we assume they'll achieve it
again & again.

Biology is a trickster though,
the coyote lurking in our marrow,
deciding our fate through slight of hand, or slight of cell.

The lesson seems to be *take nothing for granted,*
but what's being taken here is creation.

Our instinct is to preserve that
which has been stolen. Put it in a Mason jar, pickled, immune

from rot & aging. Store it in a cool & dark place,

high on an empty closet shelf.

## Tanya Berry called them *signs of evil*

but my aunt has one. A storage unit full
of sagging cardboard boxes overflowing

with Chinese plastic aircraft, fluorescent green
T-rexes, tiny Army men sharing space with a football-

shaped bank bearing the Cleveland Browns logo.
The containers all carefully labeled with my dead

cousin's name. A memorial more personal than
expensive phrasing engraved in marble.

These memories were penned by a mother's fingers,
writing her son's first name for perhaps the last time.

## Ode to the Autumn Daffodil

Amid the roadside weeds on my way home,
I spy it out the window to the right.
Growing between the trees, kudzu & loam,
its petals reflect the sun's own lemon light.

At forty miles per hour, hard to tell,
exactly what type of flower it was.
The yellow of a faded daffodil,
face open like a lily or an iris.

This time of year though, only goldenrod
speckles these hills with its radiant hue,
& thus I thought my vision surely flawed
to see this sunny capturer of dew.

The next day I returned & looking back,
found a weathered Dollar General sack.

# Appalachian Back Road at 30 MPH

I saw the rabbit's sandy limb
jerk. Death twitch? Last ditch effort
to peel itself off asphalt
& into dying grass & leaves, now brake-

light red? I stop, thankful
for no tailgaters, look
through the back glass
for evidence of breath,
but the beige body wisps
listless in the wind—

a weighted grocery sack,
stuck atop amber median
lines; on its oil-based underbelly
flaps the blood-red branding.

## Paradelle for Natty Light *

The cobalt blue letters peer out.
The cobalt blue letters peer out.
Their white box sits awry in a ditch.
Their white box sits awry in a ditch.
In a ditch sits awry, the white letters
peer out their cobalt blue box.

The cardboard now punctured with holes.
The cardboard now punctured with holes.
Red & gold logos appear as torn medals.
Red & gold logos appear as torn medals.
Gold & punctured as cardboard medals,
the red logos now appear torn with holes.

The Natural Light case perhaps may be vacant.
The Natural Light case perhaps may be vacant.
But impressions are not always truths.
But impressions are not always truths.
Light impressions are not always vacant,
but natural truths perhaps may be the case.

Red, white & blue truths may be vacant,
perhaps not always as gold medals appear.
Logos are now natural, their letters, but cardboard
impressions, peer out. The ditch,
torn with holes, punctured, sits awry.
The cobalt light, a box in the case.

* "Natty Light" is slang for Natural Light beer.

# Fur-lorn

## I.

Your bark-hued fur spackled
the road on my grocery run,
your innards pulled outards,
a feast for the carrion-eaters.

Tire tracks, black across your road-
rashed back & nearby splatters
share how bits & pieces of you
affix to rubber, to undercarriage.

## II.

500 feet from your corpse, two muddy
truck tires stack next to candy & Nabs
wrappers—a found sculpture amid the gravel-
hewn pull-off. I wonder how many creatures'

cells these tires have spread, parked
ironically next to a PLEASE DON'T
LITTER sign staked in the high grass.
So much is at stake in our human

takeover of the planet. On my morning
grocery run, I saw blue pinwheels
by the hundreds staked into government
building front lawns, meant to raise

awareness of child abuse or maybe
to prevent it, but what's preventing
these pinwheels from landing in a land-
fill next to the county auditor election

signs, the lilac-colored bows adorning
the bridge's light poles for undisclosed
reasons, the Starbucks cups emptied
of their overpriced caffeinated contents?

III.

Sycamore balls litter my back
yard, their marshmallow centers
oozing nougat-like if they fall

hard enough to the cobblestone
pavers. The tulip poplar—which isn't
really a poplar at all—gifts petals

tie-dyed orange, white & lime
lining the walkway between house
& shed like a wedding aisle.

IV.

The groundhog doesn't need
these words. They are human-
formed & for. Our cells, like
microplastics, stretch county-wide.

# Along Cope Creek Rd.

Someone staked signs—
white with red sans

serif lettering: PLEASE DON'T
LITTER. As though their signs don't

serve to remind drivers-by that the grass
is owned & the scenery marred

by signs just as much as litter,
even if that wasn't the grass owner's

intent, even if the owner of the grass
views signs as art & litter as garbage

because we are taught to value art
but not garbage but never taught

to distinguish between the two
or distinguish how one

can own art & garbage
& signs & grass

that stand beside the road,
another's intentions staked into it.

## Easter Sunday in the South

I don my gloves, fetch
my bag, brain-gray
with a navy Food Lion
logo. Beside the road,

I find the filters—
2 Marlboro Lights, 1 Pall Mall,
3 unidentifiable, shredding
to white & yellow fluff.

1 styrofoam clamshell
& its accompanying checkered
liner lingering nearby—both
fill my sack alongside paper

napkins, a red Purina dog
treat pouch, an airplane bottle
devoid of its liquid contents,
a white & yellow Bojangles bag.

My neighbors don their suits
& dresses patterned with purple flowers
like the violets by my feet. These folks
are headed to church; I am already there.

## Weekly Worship at the City Dump

Every second Sunday, come
gather amid prophets' decayed condoms underfoot.

Look upward eyes shut; let us pray
toward papermill billows pretending they're clouds.

If there are crowds, sit on canine-gnawed couches,
their cheap orange velvet scuffed threadless. The reclining

makeshift pew springs on the chosen few
stigmata through its papery upholstery. You will

be cleansed by your blood. Communion's
tin can chalices runneth over with acid rainwater

spiced with leaf matter & loam.
If you wish to be saved, this is the price.

Outside, without a kiln
to bake proper wafers, bread heels suffice.

Close your eyes so you are blind
to the hollows rat-sized meals & mold have left behind.

The birth story's sacred virgin, a revelation:
discarded Ortho Tri-Cyclen packs, 6 robin-shell & jaundice-hued pills

left intact. Here the crucifix is a marred child's doll
with syringes tacked to scrap plywood with upward appendages.

# Holy Temple of Restoration, Pikeville, KY

inhabits an old storefront, peddling
righteousness & an afterlife
brimming with mansions *in the sky,*
*Lord, in the sky.* Right down the block,

gas stations sell Mother Mary
scented candles, crimson like her
son's bloodshed, stocked
beside dusty Snickers & Milky Way

bars. Treats for bribing children
to sit through Sunday's sermon, to scrub
communion wafers' bland flecks
from their unknowing tongues.

# 13 Miles South of Louisa, KY

sits an electric spool
bracing a power line. Emblazoned
in '80s jazzercise orange,
a notice: *This is fiber—not copper.*

A warning to any would-be thieves
slinging precious metal for change
to cover daycare costs or light bills.

The spool is labeled as electric
company property, but aren't we all?

The fossil fuel industry,
a dealer with scarred mountains
instead of arms; dirty
creeks instead of needles.

Yet the blame is laid
on people labeled thieves
who are reclaiming power

through their own hands,
their fists full & raised.

# Power Dynamic, May 2023

Hours ago, Oklo, Inc. shared
plans for Piketon, Ohio, to grow
both of its next-generation
clean power nuclear fission plants.
The return of jobs for its two
thousand residents, the paper's

digital print implies. The siting papers
are filed & soon Oklo's shares
priced at ten cents apiece will be two
dollars or more. Stocks growing
pockets fatter as the fields' plants
are stripped for this next generation.

The parents of this generation
filed affidavits, talked to local papers,
exposed how the A-plant's
practices endangered their lives. They shared
their cancer screening results, growths
invading thyroid glands, rates nearly two

times the national average. Two
miles from the old site, a generation
went to middle school, their growing
bodies subjected to U-235, the newspapers
report. But word of mouth shared
their stories decades before, tales implanted

like misplaced cells, explanted
by doctors, who divide tissue into two
sections for biopsy. The bad news shared
over & over with each new generation.
We carry our diagnoses on folded papers,
their scientific terms don't excise the growths

spreading in our organs. Yet growth
is always promoted. We want our plants—
knee-high corn, emerald soybean, paper
mills—to be better, stronger, available for two
or three or more future generations
so they might have prosperity to share.

Kudzu is an invasive growth on Ohio farmland. Two
hundred years ago, plants were sold to a generation
who believed its papery leaves & sweet blossoms worth sharing.

# Jesus, Radioactive Headmaster

*A Christian ministry with ties to the nuclear industry plans to convert the recently auctioned Zahn's Corner Middle School into a STEM-based Christian charter school, sparking outrage and concern among local residents and activists,* Piketon, OH, August 2024

Ministry leaders claimed to be tugged
by the spirit            perhaps one of their own

invention            not one of their fellow humans
who invented the atom bomb            but the source

of the bombs                        those STEM fields the
church  claims
to amplify.            Their acting goal            to worship

Christ through generating            a new generation,
Neptunium-237-afflicted                        but able to
understand

their God-given mission.

# Data Center Duplex

*New Day Data Centers, a recently-formed entity with no online presence, proposed to build a new data center at the site of the former uranium enrichment plant near Piketon, Ohio, according to David Forster of WOUB on December 2, 2025.*

The Scioto River curls south through Pike County,
where its waters cooled three A-plant towers for decades.

> Now it may cool servers & racks for decades,
> as data centers generate continuous heat.

Developers seem to be in a continuous heat,
thrusting themselves upon flat tracts of land.

> Erecting steel structures upon flat tracts of land
> like the flags they'd implant, making land claims

in places where people are already planted, spaces already claimed,
as though Manifest Destiny applies to data sets & electronic records.

> But the people of Piketon have data sets & electronic records
> correlating cancer clusters to corporate contamination.

Across the nation, waters bear corporate contamination.
So, too, does the Scioto as it curls south through Pike County.

# The Mighty Ohio

I.

The coal
        the coal
              it sinks to the catfish
mouths, shovel & shut, shovel
          & shut, spooning in
rocks & sticks & A-plant runoff.

II.

The barges'
          twisted steel would sell
      well at the Circleville scrap yards,
but it would have to be salvaged

first. My sister took a selfie,
          her shadow lurking like a ghost
    on the murky river's surface. A somber, small reflection
painted in oil & gas. My parents warned us

              not to wade in. I asked if fish
would gobble up my toes, like the 6 footers
        caught in Paint Creek.

III.

Dad chuckled, *There aren't any fish in there, Jess.*
He used to fix tracks for the C&O. Drove
heavy equipment across the river's bridge spans. Recalls
              barges on fire & smoke like the Cuyahoga up north.

IV.

But the EPA made it a-okay, the local
              newspapers say & coal keeps the lights on,
as the slogan goes, so nobody cares
                                what enters catfish holes.

## Bodies for the Birds

Vultures silently separate
muscle from sinew
ligament from bone
cartilage from skin.
Absent a syrinx, these creatures
scavenge, stealthy as night
shown in their feathers.
Their creator knowing
such purification
rituals
should be solemn.

# About the Author

Jessica Cory is the editor of *Appalachian Journal: A Regional Studies Review,* published since 1972 at Appalachian State University. She holds a PhD in Native American, African American, and environmental literatures from the University of North Carolina at Greensboro and is the editor of *Mountains Piled upon Mountains: Appalachian Nature Writing in the Anthropocene* (WVU Press, 2019) and the co-editor (with Laura Wright) of *Appalachian Ecocriticism and the Paradox of Place* (UGA Press, 2023). Her creative and scholarly writings have been published in the *North Carolina Literary Review, North Dakota Quarterly, Northern Appalachia Review,* and other fine publications.

S
Sheila-Na-Gig Editions

www.ingramcontent.com/pod-product-compliance
Ingram Content Group UK Ltd.
Pitfield, Milton Keynes, MK11 3LW, UK
UKHW042011190726
13854UKWH00005B/2245